A–Z
of
JAMAICAN
PATOIS
(PATWAH)

A-Z
of
JAMAICAN
PATOIS
(PATWAH)

Words, Phrases and how we use them.

TERESA P. BLAIR, Ph.D.

authorHOUSE®

AuthorHouse™ LLC
1663 Liberty Drive
Bloomington, IN 47403
www.authorhouse.com
Phone: 1-800-839-8640

Published by AuthorHouse   07/18/2013

ISBN: 978-1-4817-5234-3 (sc)
ISBN: 978-1-4817-5235-0 (e)

Library of Congress Control Number: 2013908843

Introduction

The inspiration to write this book came from an email I received. The email, captioned—Patois is a Language, stated that a company could not fill vacant positions advertised by the company, because most of the applicants failed the interviews which were conducted in Patois. The company, which advertised for people who could speak Patois, did state that the interviews would be conducted in Patois.

According to the email, many of the interviewees were born in Jamaica, or were born outside of Jamaica, by Jamaican parents. Although they met the other qualifications necessary for the vacant positions, they could not speak the dialect required to land them the positions. One of these candidates was the daughter of the person from whom the email chain originated.

I have been asked several times about how to speak Patois, and whether Patois is a written language. Hence, this book is not just for all those who speak some Patois, but for those who want to learn how to speak Patois, and for those who are just curious about the dialect. Included in this group, are those who migrated from Jamaica at an early age, children of Jamaican parents born outside of Jamaica, those who want to reconnect with their Jamaican heritage (roots), and for those visitors and/or tourists who would like to understand or speak some Patois during their visit.

Further, this book is also written to inform readers that Patois is indeed a written language. It is spoken in every nation or country where descendants or natives of Jamaica reside, whether through birth or migration. Notably, Patois is spoken in the United Kingdom, the United States, Canada, Belize, France, Ethiopia, and in several other countries and islands. Plays, songs, and movies are written in Patois.

It is my hope that this book will keep Patois alive. Its users should not forget however, that English is the main language of Jamaica. Patois—a combination of African, French and English, is a sub-language or dialect. The words and terms used here, do by know means exhaust those of the dialect. However, they are enough to teach the user how to speak Jamaican patois.

This book does not necessarily contain the Patois slangs used by the Jamaican Rastafarians or the younger "up and coming" Jamaican population who seem to be expanding the vocabulary of the dialect.

A

Abraad or Abroad: Refers to a country or place outside of Jamaica. (See foreign.)

1. Yu ear seh Lyn daata gone abroad? (Did you hear that Lyn's daughter is gone abroad?) 2. Mose a we nurse dem gone abroad. (Most of our nurses are gone abroad.)

Ackie: Means—ackee, which is Jamaica's national fruit.

1. Me a cook some ackie an salfish fe breckfass. (I am cooking some ackee and saltfish for breakfast.) 2. De lunch special fe de day a ackie an salfish. (The lunch special for the day is ackee and saltfish.)

A fe: Is used for—it is for; it's for; or it belongs to. Shows possession.

1. A fe me luggige. (It is my luggage.) 2. A no fe me. (It is or it's not mine.)

A go: Means—I am going to. Expresses aim, purpose, intent, or determination.

1. Me a go to bed now. (I am going to bed now.) 2. Me a go tell him dat me sarry. (I am going to tell him that I am sorry.)

Aise: Refers to the human or animal ear or ears.

1. Dat man as some big aise. (That man has some big ears.) 2. De goat ha only one aise. (The goat has only one ear.)

A it mek: Means—that is why. Used to show a reason for something or for a happening.

1. A it mek yu fail yu exam. (That is the reason you failed your examination.) 2. A it mek yu no go no weh. (That is why you are not allowed to go anywhere.)

Aal: Means—all.

1. Aal a uno come inside. (All of you, come inside.) 2. Me sell im aal a de sugarcane. (I sold him all of the sugarcane.)

An: It is used for—on or and.

1. She sittin an de chair. (She is sitting on the chair). 2. Him an me a fren. (He and I are friends.)

Anneda: It is used for—another.

1. Please ge me annada chance. (Please give me another chance.)

2. She ha anneda baby. (She has another baby.)

Ard: It is used for—hard. Here the "h" is eliminated as in the word "hard". Shows difficulty, harshness, rigidity, or toughness.

1. De dirt ard fe dig. (The dirt or ground is hard to dig.) 2. De boot dem ard, and a

queeze me feet. (These boots are hard, or tough, and are squeezing my feet.)

Argie: Is used for argue. To argue or quarrel with.

1. Me no argie wid lickle girls. (I do not argue with little girls.) 2. De bwoy is very argiementitive. (The boy is very argumentative.)

Aringe: It is used for—orange, a popular Jamaican citrus fruit.

1. Buy de arringe, dem sweet. (Buy the orange because they are sweet.) 2. Im ave a big arringe farm. (He has a big orange farm.)

Arr: Means—her. The pronoun her.

1. Arr madda say dat she caan go. (Her mother says that she cannot go.) 2. Arr son get de scholarship. (Her son got the scholarship.)

Arredy: Means—already.

1. Dem gone arredy. (They are gone already.) 2. Me buy de shoes arredy. (I have bought the shoes already.)

Arright: It is used for—all right.

1. Yu arright? (Are you all right?) 2. Yes, me arright. (Yes, I am all right.)

As: Means—has. It is used as a verb and not as a preposition.

1. She as arr uniform fe school arready. (She has her uniform for school already.)

2. Im ha im shirt tun wrang side out. (He has his shirt turn wrong side out.)

At, Ed, Enry—are other words that lose the "H" in some conversations. **At** is used for hat; **ed** for head; and **Enry** for Henry.

1. Enry put de at pan im ed. (Henry puts the hat on his head.) 2. Im put Enry's at

pan im ed. (He puts Henry's hat on his head.)

Ave: It is used for—have.

1. Me no ave aal de money. (I do not have all the money.) 2. Dem ave ole eep a lan. (They have a whole heap or huge acreage of land.)

Axe: Means—ask.

1. Yes, me axe arr bout it. (Yes, I asked her about it.) 2. Why yu axsin me? (Why are you asking me?)

B

Backkle (or boccle): Is used for—bottle.

1. Mine yu brock de backkle. (Be careful not to break the bottle.) 2. Please full de boccle wid waata. (Please fill the bottle with water.)

Badda me: Means—worry, worrying, or used to show comparison.

1. Wah mek yu a badda me so? (Why are you worrying me so much?) 2. Noh badda go, it too late now. (Do not worry to go, it is too late now.) 3. Fe arr son badda dan fe me. (Her son's behavior is worse than my son's.)

Bam or Baps: Means—suddenly or immediately.

1. Jus as she a tell me say arr puppy run weh, baps, dare it was. (Just as she was telling me that her puppy ran away, suddenly, there it was.) 2. Im cum out a

jail jus week, an bam, im gaan right back in deh. (He came out of jail last week, and immediately he is back in jail).

Bassman: Is used for—boss. Also affectionately used to address a friend or relative.

1. Bassman, gi me a money noh. (Boss, give some money.) 2. Me kudden tell when las me se yu bassman. (I couldn't tell when was the last time I saw you boss or friend.)

Batten: Is used for—baton.

1. Look deh! Im drap de batten. (Look at that! He dropped the baton.) 2. A hope dem pass de batten good dis time. (I hope that they pass the baton well this time.)

Bawl: It is used to describe loud crying. Usually a sense of loss or grief.

1. Lard, she baal fi arr faada a de funeral? (Lord, she wept or cried a lot at the

funeral, for her father.) 2. Wa mek de baby a baal so? (Why is the baby crying so loudly?)

Bax or Box: Means—to hit in or across the face.

1. No mek me bax /box yu. (Don't let me hit you in the face.) 2. De boy bax me. (The boy hit me in or across my face.)

Ben deh: It is used for the verbs—has, have been, was.

1. Yu know dat she ben deh a abroad since last year? (Did you know that she has been living abroad since last year?) 2. No sah, me tink she ben deh yah aal de time. (No sir, I thought that she was (or has been) living here all the time.)

Betta: Means—better. It is also used to show comparison.

1. Fi me soup hav a betta flava dan de one fram de restaurant. (My soup has

a better flavor than the one from the restaurant.) 2. She feelin betta teday dan yesseday. (She is feeling better today than yesterday.)

Bosey: Describes a proud, or boastful person.

1. Dat deh gal too bosey. (That girl is too proud or boastful.) 2. She married dat bosey bwoy fram Kingston. (She married that boastful boy from Kingston.)

Bout: Means—about.

1. Did yu hear bout de plane dat crash? (Did you hear about the plane that crashed?) 2. Yu go bout yu business, an leave me alone. (You go about your business and leave me alone.)

Brackra: Is used for—master, wealthy employer, rich person.

1. De brackra haase dem pretty. (The master's horses are pretty.) 2. De brackra

dem wok yu to det, an no pay yu much fe u time. (The rich people work you to death, and do not pay you much for your time.)

Bredda: Used to show—kinship, or sometimes close friendships.

1. Dat one is Susie bredda by arr faada. (That one is Suzie's brother by her father.)
2. Dis man is me true bredda. (This man is my true brother.)

Bruk: Means—broke. Indicates one is without money, or the breakage of an object.

1. Me bruk man. Money done. (I am broke. My money is finished.) 2. Mine yu bruk de glaas. (Be careful not to break the glass.)

Bud: Means—bird. Also used for the bud of a plant.

1. De bud mek ness ina de barn roof. (The bird made a nest in the roof of the barn.)

2. De mango tree a bud. (The mango tree is budding.)

Bwilin or Bwile: These are used for—boiling, boil, or to get angry.

1. Is de waata bwilin yet? (Is the water boiling as yet?) 2. Me temper a bwile. (My temper is boiling, or I am getting very angry.)

Bwoy: Means—boy. A young man. Sometimes it is derogatively used for a grown man who the user does not respect.

1. Weh de bwoy a do so long? (What is the boy doing so long? What is taking the boy so long?) 2. Yu bwoy, no talk to me ooman again. (You boy, do not talk to my woman [wife or girlfriend] again).

C

Cawfe: Means—coffee.

1. Please sell me a cup of hat cawfe. (Please sell me a cup of hot coffee.) 2. Dis ya cawfe too cole. (This coffee is too cold.)

Cerfitikit: Means—a certificate.

1. Me son graduate collige and gat im cerfitikit lass week. (My son graduated from college and got his certificate last week.) 2. Mek me see yu cerfitikit. (Let me see your certificate).

Chaklick or chaclit: Is used for—Chocolate. Native homemade product similar to cocoa.

1. Me love me chaklick tea fi brockfass in de maanings. (I love my chocolate tea for breakfast in the mornings). 2. Yu ave hat chaclit? (Do you have hot chocolate?)

Check yu: Means to notice or to pay special attention to you. To see you.

1.Dat bwoy a check yu out. (That boy is noticing or paying special attention to you.) 2. Me wi com check yu layta. (I will come to see you later.)

Chuck: It is used for—truck.

1. A wha ina de chuck? (What is in the truck, or what is the truck carrying?)
2. Did Sammy buy anneda chuck? (Did Sammy buy another truck?)

Clawt: Means—cloth. Material used to make clothing.

1. Yu buy de clawt fe de pickney unifarm? (Did you buy the cloth for the child's uniform?) 2. Me noh get the clawt fe mek Susie unifarm. (I did not get the cloth to make Susie's uniform.)

Cobard: It is used for—cupboard.

1. De cup ina de cobard. (The cup is in the cupboard.) 2. Yu need to clean out de cobard. (You need to clean out the cupboard.)

Coconat: Means—coconut.

1. Coconat ile give it a betta flava. (Coconut oil gives it a better flavor.) 2. Me no use coconut ile fe cook it atall. (I do not use coconut oil to cook it at all.)

Cole: Means—coal or cold. It is used interchangeably with the decrease in temperature and charcoal.

1.Kaase de weather change so aftin, me hav a cole. (Because the weather changes so often, I have a cold.) 2. Careful dat yu no step pon de live cole. (Be careful that you do not step on the burning charcoal.)

Coodeh: It is used for—Look at that! Denotes an element of surprise.

1. Coodeh! De dankey drap ina de hole. (Look at that! The donkey fell into the hole.) 2. Coodeh! Im drap de batten aggen. (Look at that! He dropped the baton again.)

Cooyah: Means—Look at this! To draw attention to.

1. Cooyah, de milk spwile. (Look at this, the milk is spoilt. 2. Now, cooyah! she tink she all dat. (Now, look at this! she thinks that she is all that.)

Cris: Means that—something or someone looks very good, or very beautiful.

1. De bredda hah waan cris chick. (The brother has a very good looking girl.) 2. Yu se de cris ooman im marry? (Do you see the beautiful woman he married?)

Cum yah: Means—come here.

1. Me seh cum yah. (I say come here.) 2. Tell im fi micase an cum yah. (Tell him to make haste and come here).

Cu pan: Means—look at. Sometimes used derogatively.

1. Cu pan yu! (Look at you!) 2. Cu pan yu to! (Look at you to!) (Derogatively used)

Cyaan: Means—cannot or can't.

1. Me cyaan salve dis yah mats problem atall. (I cannot solve this math problem at all.) 2. She cyaan come to de party. (She can not come to the party.)

D

Dat: Used for that.

1. Dat a noh fe me. (That is not for me, or that is not mine). 2. Yu noh aall dat. (You are not all that.)

Dat deh: Means—that is, or that, when used in disgust. (See Deh)

1. Dat deh man a get pon me nerve. (That man is getting on my nerve.) 2. Me noh no wheh dat deh sinting deh. (I don't know where that thing is.)

Dawg: Is used for—dog.

1.What a big dawg? (What a big dog?) 2. Yu lie wid dawgs yu ketch flea. (If you lay with dogs, you will catch flea.)

Dawta: Means—daughter, the female child of a parent, or sometimes for a female lover—not a wife.

1. She a Danny's dawta. (She is Danny's daughter [female child].) 2. Noh touch arr, a fi me dawta. (Don't touch her, she is my lover.)

De: Is used for—the.

1. Yes sah, yu a de baas. (Yes sir, you are the boss.) 2. De moon a shine bright tenite. (The moon is shining brightly tonight.)

Deesent: It is used to denote good behavior or character.

1. Dat is a deesent girl. (That is a well behaved girl.) 2. She married a deesent man. (She married a man of good character.)

Deh: Is used for the verbs—are, was, were.

1. Weh dem deh now? (Where are they now?) 2. Please tell im wey we ben deh.

2. (Please tell him where we were.)

Deh Deh: Means—there.

1. She no deh deh. (She is not there.) 2. Me come all dis way fe seeim, an im no deh deh. (I came all this way to see him, and he is not there.)

Deh pan: It is used for—the preposition on.

1. It dehpan de table. (It is on the table.) 2. Me dehpan a strick diet now. (I am on a strict diet now.)

Dem: It is used for—the pronouns they and them.

1. Dem gone to de party. (They are gone to the party.) 2. She noh like wha dem done to de house. (She does not like what they did to the house.)

De marrows: Means—tomorrow or in the morning.

1. Inna de marrows den. (See you tomorrow then.) 2. Dem a com inna de

20

marrows. (They will be coming in the morning.)

Dem-deh: Is used for—the pronoun those.

1. Dem-deh bwoy no know dat dem late fe school? (Those boys don't know that they are late for school?) 2. Dem-deh parents mek dem pickney rule dem. (Those parents allow their children to rule them.)

Dere: Means—there. Used to show position.

1. Dem ova dere. (They are over there.) 2. Me naan go ova dere. (I am not going over there.)

Do or Du: Means—to beg, or to ask pleadingly. Please. I beg you.

1. Do mommy, noh beat me. (I beg you mommy, don't spank me.) 2. Du, noh stay too long. (Please, do not stay too long.)

Drap: Is used for—drop or drops. To drop something.

1. Yu feel de rain drap? (Did you feel the rain drops?) 2. Noh drap de ball. (Do not drop the ball.)

Dun: It is used for—done, to finish, or to be finished with.

1. Yu noh dun yet? (Aren't you finished yet?) 2. Me dun arredy. (I am already finished.)

Dung: It is used interchangeably for the adverb down, and the feces of animals such as cows and goats.

1. De ball roll dung de hill. (The ball rolled down the hill.) 2. Cow dung a good manure fe de plants. (Cow feces make good manure for the plants.)

Duppy: Means—ghost. Also used to described an "ugly" person.

1. She sa dat she se a duppy ina de house. (She said that she saw a ghost in the house.) 2. Lef me alone, yu faavah duppy. (Leave me alone, you look like a ghost.)

Dutty: Means—dirty, unclean, or not of a good character.

1. Go change dat dutty shirt. (Go and change that dirty shirt.) 2.Yu dating dat deh dutty gal? (Are you dating that girl who has no character?)

Dweit or Dweet: It is used for—do it, or to do.

1. Me caan dweit. (I cannot do it.) 2. Me sista wi ha fi dweet fe me. (My sister will have to do it for me.)

E

Edicasion: Means—education. Usually refers to college degree or degrees.

1. She gat a good edicasion. (She has a good education.) 2. Aal im pickney dem gat good edicasion. (All his children have good education.)

Eeen-hi: Means—yes, I understand, or agree.

1. Eeen hi, me ear yu man. (Yes, I hear or understand you man.)

2. Eeen hi, mi we go fi you. (Yes, I will go for you.)

Ef: Is used for—the conjunction if.

1. Ef me noh pass me tess, me caan goh pan de bus trip. (If I do not pass my test, I cannot go on the bus trip.) 2. Yu wi pass de tess ef yu study. (You will pass the test if you study.)

Ello: Means—hello! Usually when answering the telephone.

1. Ello! Ms. Green speaking. (Hello, this is Ms Green speaking.)

2. Ello! Ooh is caaling? (Hello, who is calling?)

Eva: It is used for—ever.

1. Eva since arr madda dead, she no speak to no wan. (Ever since her mother died, she has not spoken to anyone.) 2. A will nat talk to dat man eva again. (I will not talk to that man ever again.)

F

Faada: Means—father, or a male parent.

1. Dat man a Micky faada. (That man is Micky's father.)

2. Mi faada no want mi fe talk to yu. (My father does not want me to talk to you.)

Faass: Means—feisty. Also used to describe movements, as in moving fast.

1. Me no talk to arr, cause she too faass. (I do not [don't] talk to her, because she is too feisty. 2. Dat bwoy can run very faass. (That boy can run very fast.)

Face-ty: Means—feisty.

1. Dat lickle gal too face-ty man! (That little girl is feisty man!) 2. A wan face-ty ooman dat deh. (That is one feisty woman.)

Fambly: Means—family or people who are related to one another.

1. Yu faada an me a fambly. (Your father and I are related to each other.) 2. She come fram a big fambly. (She is a member of, or comes from, a large family.)

Fareign or Farin: Refers to any country or place outside of Jamaica.

1. Me dawtas come fram fareign lass night. (My daughters came from foreign, [or from abroad] last night.) 2. Aal a dem fareigners just come fram fareign. (All those foreigners [people] just came from another country.)

Farrid: means—forehead.

1. De ball lick im pon im farrid. (The ball hit him on his forehead.) 2. What a big farrid dat deh man ha? (What a big forehead that man has?)

Fe: It is used for—for or to.

1. A fe me. (It is, or it's for me.) 2. Me ha fe go get me madda a de bus tap. (I have to go and get my mother at the bus stop.)

Fe-de-road: Means—before I go.

1. Gi me a hug fe-de-road. (Give ma a hug before I go.) 2. Fix me anneda drink fe-de-road. (Fix me another drink before I go.)

Fenkeh fenkeh: Means—weak, unaggressive, or slow.

1. Dat deh man too fenkeh fenkeh fe me. (That man is too weak or unaggressive for me.) 2. Hurry up gal. Yu too fenkeh fenkeh. (Hurry up girl, you are too slow.)

Fi-ah: It is used for—fire.

1. De soup hat lacka fiah. (The soup is as hot as fire.) 2. Go get some wood fe de fiah. (Go and get some wood for the fire).

Flim: Means—film. It is also used for movie.

1. Me go watch a flim at the tater last night. (I went to see a movie at the theater last night.) 2. Me need some flim fe me camera. (I need some film for my camera.)

Fling: Means—to throw something.

1. Noh fling de paypa inna de ribba. (Do not throw the paper in the river.) 2. Wah mek yu fling arr book inna de wata to wet it up? (Why did you throw her book into the water to make it get wet?)

Fram:—Means—from.

1. Yu jus a come fram school? (Are you just coming from school?)

2. Weh yu a come fram? (Where are you coming from?)

Fren: Is used for—friend.

1. A me fren dat. (That is my friend.)

2. A me bredda fren dem. (They are my brother's friends.)

Im ha sum pretty flowas inna im gorden

G

Gaan: Means—gone.

1. She gaan a church. (She is gone to church.) 2. Me no know weh she gaan. (I do not know where she is gone.)

Gal: Means—girl, or used derogatively for woman.

1. Me no want no relationship wid dat deh gal. (I don't want a relationship with that ill charactered girl.) 2. De gal ha five pickney arredy. (The woman has five children already.)

Galang: It is used interchangeably for—going on and go along.

1. A wah mek she a galang soh? (Why is she going on or behaving like that?) 2. Me a galang now. (I am going along now.)

Ganja: It is used for—marijuana.

1. De pohlice ketch dem wid ganja. (The police caught them with marijuana.) 2. De fareigners tink dat ganja legal in Jamaica. (The foreigners think that marijuana use is legal in Jamaica.)

Gat: Means—got. Also used for has.

1. Arr usban gat nuff money. (Her husband has lots of money.) 2. Me gat de parcel yesseday. (I got the parcel yesterday.)

Gellup: Means—gallop.

1. Dat haase kan gellup fasser dan aal de adders. (That horse can gallop faster than all the others.) 2. De bwoy can gellup like a haase. (The boy can run as fast as a horse.)

Gimme: Means—give me.

1. Gimme de cup before yu spill de cawfe. (Give me the cup before you spill the coffee.) 2. Me faada gwine gimme de

money fe buy de shoes. (My father is going to give me the money to buy the shoes.)

Ginnal: Is used for—deceiver or trickster.

1. Yu believe dat deh ginnal? (Do you believe that deceiver?) 2. Me no know wah mek she wooda fren dat deh ginnal. (I don't know why she would be-friend that trickster.)

Godeh: Means—to go or going there.

1. Look! Me naan godeh. (Look! I am not going there.) 2. If yu godeh an get trap, blame yuself. (If you go there and get trapped, then blame yourself.)

Gorden/Gordon: Used for—garden.

1. Jean gat some beautiful flowers in arr gorden. (Jean has some beautiful flowers in her garden.) 2. Missa Gardon really tek good care af im gordon. (Mr. Gordon really takes good care of his garden.)

Gooup or **Goup:** Means—to go up or going up.

1. Me a goup dey tomarraw. (I am going up there tomorrow.) 2. Me seh yu nuffi gooup deh. (I say you are not to go up there.)

Gravalishus: Means greedy or craven.

1. Laad! de little bwoy is so gravalishus. (Lord! the little boy is so greedy.)

2. Im so gravalishus, he could eat a cow. (He is so greedy, he could eat a cow.)

Gwine: Means—going or going to.

1. Me gwine tell im seh me no interested ina im. (I am going to tell him that I am not interested in him.) 2. She gwine to give a speech a de gradruasion. (She is going to give a speech at the graduation ceremony.

H

Hab or hav: It is used for—the verbs has, have, or got.

1. She no hab de money fe pay yu. (She does not have the money to pay you.) 2. Gi im whateva money yu hav. (Give him whatever money you got or have.)

Ha fe: Means—have to or must.

1. Me hafi go ina town tomarrow. (I have to go into the town tomorrow.) 2. Wah mek yu hafi swear so much? (Why must you swear so much?)

Hampa: Means—hamper(s)—large baskets placed on a donkey or mule to transport goods.

1. Dem deh hampa too big fi dat deh dankey fi carry. (Those hampers are too big for that donkey to carry.) 2. Put de hampas pan de dankey. (Put the hampers on the donkey.)

Han: Means—hand.

1. Move yu han fram onda deh. (Move your hand from under there.) 2. Yu nuffy mek yu lef han know weh yu right han a do. (You must not let your left hand know what your right hand is doing.)

Hangle: Means—handle. It is used interchangeably for to manage, and the handle of a container, like a pot or cup.

1. She knows how fi hangle arr business. (She knows how to handle her business.)

2. Hold de cup by the hangle, kaase it hat. (Hold the cup by the handle, because it's hot.)

Hard aise or **Ard aise:** Means—to be stubborn or to not listen.

1. Dat lickle pickney very ard aise. (That little child is very stubborn). 2. De dankey is hard aise, so yu haffi beat im. (The donkey is stubborn, so you will have to beat him.)

Hat: Used to describe heat or pain, as in a headache. (See **At**)

1. Be careful, de pat hangle hat. (Be careful, the pot handle is hot.)

2. Oh! me ed a hat me. (Oh! my head is paining or hurting me.)

Hole heap: Means—lots of, or many.

1. Hole heap a bwoy pak up inna de car. (Many boys are packed into the car.) 2. Im parence ha hole heap a money. (His parents have lots of money.)

A hole heap a money dat.

I

Ile: Means—oil.

1. Put some ile pan it. (Put some oil on it.)
2. Me prefa fe cook wid coconat ile, dan de other ile dem. (I prefer to cook with coconut oil than all the other oils.)

Im:—Used for—him or he.

1. Im no know sa me deh ya. (He does not know that I am here.) 2. She sa she like im. (She says that she likes him.)

Ina or Inna: Used for—in or into.

1. De gal sidong ina the house all day. (The girl sits in the house all day.) 2. Look inna de gordon yu we fine it. (Look into the garden and you will find it.)

Intaruptid: Means—interrupted or to interupt.

1. De nize intaruptid me sleep. (The noise interrupted my sleep [or woke me up].)
2. Shh! No intarup me aggen. (Shh! Don't interrupt me again.)

Irie: Refers to, or is used for something that is good, great, or excellent.

1. De music is irie. (The music is good, or great, or excellent.) 2.Me feeling irie. (I am feeling good, great or excellent.)

J

Jah: Used for—Jehovah or God mainly in the Rasta religion.)

1. Jah will provide. (God will provide.) 2. Jah no like dem kine a doings. (God does not like those kinds of things.)

Jam: Means—trouble or difficulty.

1. Bwoy! Me ina a little money jam right off ya now. (Boy! I am in a little money trouble at this moment.) 2. When me get out a de jam, me will pay yu everyting. (When I get out of this financial difficulty, I will pay you everything.)

Jam Dung or Jamdum: Affectionately used for—Jamaica.

1. All road lead to Jam Dung fe de independence. (All roads lead to Jamaica for its independence celebration.) 2. Some a de bess beaches inna Jamdum. (Some of the best beaches are in Jamaica.)

Jessum Piece! It is used for the phrase—that's wonderful! or gosh!

1. Jessum piece! Me daata pass arr exam. (It is so wonderful! My daughter has passed her examination.) 2. Jessum piece! wey yu a badda me fa? (Gosh! why are you bothering me?)

Jancro: Means—john crow—the name given to a vulture or scavenger bird. It is also used to describe a worthless person during an angry rage or quarrel.

1. Wan animal dead anda de tree whe de jancro dem deh. (An animal is dead under the tree where the scavengers/vultures are.) 2. Me no waan dat deh jancro near me. (I do not want that worthless person near me.)

Se de jancro deh

K

Kaaf/Kaafing: Means—cough or coughing.

1. She kaafing like a dog. (She is coughing like a dog.) 2. De kaafing intaruptid me sleep. (The coughing interrupted my sleep.)

Kaan/Kawn—Means—corn. It is used interchangeably with the grain (corn grain) and the old method of preserving meat using salt and pepper.

1. Me get a good kawn crop this ear. (I got a good corn crop this year.) 2. De kaan pork mek the soup rich. (The corned pork adds richness to the soup.)

Kantaminated: Means—contaminated.

1. The helt department people seh dat de waata is kantaminated. (The health department people said that the water is contaminated.) 2. No trow de gabige

inna de pon, caase it we kantaminate it. (Do not throw the garbage in the pond, because it will cause it to be contaminated.)

Kauz or **Kaase:** Used for—because or your fault.

1. Me neva go, kauz me wake up late. (I did not go, because I woke up late.) 2. A Tommy kaase the glaas fe brock. (Tommy is the one who caused the glass to break.)

Kiaff: Means—calf or the young of a cow.

1. De cow ha wan pretty kiaff. (The cow has a pretty calf.) 2. Dat cow ha bout six kiaff now. (That cow now has approximately six calves.)

Kiar: Used for—car.

1. All a unnu caan ride inna de kiar the same time. (All of you cannot ride in the car at the same time.) 2. Im ago drive im

pupa kiar. (He is going to drive his father's car.)

Kibba: Means—to cover or cover.

1. You no know fe kibba yu mout when yu kaafing? (Don't you know that you should cover your mouth when you are coughing?) 2. Please kibba de pat fi me. (Please cover the pot for me.)

Kyarri: Used for—carry, take, or to bring.

1. Look! im a kyarri de hampa pon im ed. (Look! He is carrying the hamper on his head.) 2. Me tell yu fe kyarri de broom ova ya. (I told you to bring the broom over here.)

L

Laad: Used for—please, Oh! or Lord. It sometimes expresses a feeling of disgust. (See **Lawd**)

1. Laad maasa, tap complaining. (Please Mr.! you should stop complaining.)

2. Laad! Me neba no seh me ha fe don dis by tree a'clack? (Oh! I never knew that I would have to finish this by three o'clock?)

Laas: Means—lost. To lose an article.

1. Me lass two dalla out a me lunch money. (I have lost two dollars from my lunch money.) 2. It mossy laas, kauz me kaan fine it. (It must be lost, because I cannot find it.)

Lacka: Used for—like.

1. Wa mek yu talk to dat deh bwoy whe look lacka criminal? (Why do you talk to that boy who looks like a criminal?) 2. No,

im no look lacka dat atall. (No, he does not look like that at all.)

Lamps: Means—cheated, fooled or to make a fool of.

1. De ooman lamps me outa me money. (The woman cheated me out of my money.) 2. De bwoy a lamps yu. (The boy is making a fool of you)

Lang: Means—long.

1. A lang time me no se im (seem). (It's a long time since I have seen him.) 2. No tan too lang a de mall. (Don't stay too long at the mall.)

Lawd/Laad: Means—Lord.

1. May de Lawd ha mercy pon yu. (May the Lord have mercy on you.) 2. Lawd, help me fe finish dis by tree a'clack. (Lord, help me to finish this by three o'clock.)

Lef: Used for—leave or left, and the opposite of right.

1. Me late kaase de bus lef me. (I am late because the bus left me.) 2. She no lef yet? (She has not left as yet?) 3. Put de fork ina yu lef han, an de nife inna de right. (Put the fork in your left hand, and the knife in the right.)

Liad: Means—liar.

1. No listen to im, im a liad. (Do not listen to him, he is a liar.) 2. Dat liad gal whe aalways lie, a come. (That girl who is always telling lies, is coming.)

Lick: Used for—hit or spank.

1. Im lick me ina me ed. (He hit me in my head.) 2. Me gwaan give im a licking when im come back. (I am going to give him a spanking when he comes back.)

Lickle: Means—little or small.

1. Arr baby lickle fe im age. (Her baby is small for his age.) 2. Me no argie wid lickle girls. (I do not argue with little girls.)

M

Maawning: Means—morning.

1. Me tell im good maawning but im no ansa. (I told him good morning but he did not answer.) 2. What a lovely maawning? (What a lovely morning?)

Madda: Means—mother.

1. Me madda soon come. (My mother will be coming soon.) 2. Yu madda seh yu fe ge me de book. (Your mother says that you are to give me the book.)

Maasa: Used for—master or mister. It is also affectionately used for one's husband, friend or boss.

1. Yu no hear yu massa a call yu? (Don't you hear your boss calling you?) 2. Maasa, me kaan ge yu, a no fe me. (Friend, I cannot give it to you, it's not mine.)

Mashate/mashait: Means—machete. In Jamaica it is a cutlass.

1. Wa mek yu no use de mashate fe cut it? (Why don't you use the machete [cutlass] to cut it?) 2. Oh Lawd! Im chap de daag wid de mashait. (Oh Lord! He chopped [cut] the dog with the [cutlass] machete.)

Maskitta: Means—mosquito.

1. De dutty wata full a maskitta. (The dirty water is crowded with mosquitoes.) 2. De helt people dem spraying houses fe prevent maskitta. (The people from the health department are spraying the houses to prevent an influx of mosquitoes.)

Mawga: Used for—meager.

1. What a mawga lickle dog? (What a meager little dog?) 2. We get a mawga crop of caarn dis ear. (We got a meager crop of corn this year.)

Me—a—go: Means—I am going.

1. Me a go ina town tomarrow. (I am going into town [the city] tomorrow.) 2. Me a go tell arr fe lef me pickney alone. (I am going to tell her to leave my child alone.)

Me—ha—fe: Used for—I have to or I must.

1. Me ha fe get to de bus tap before de bus lef me. (I have to get to the bus stop before the bus leaves me.) 2. Me ha fe pay de bill tedeh before dem charge me late fee. (I must pay the bill today before I am charged a late fee.)

Mek: Means—make or let.

1. Me no know wah mek im tell su much lie. (I don 't know what makes him tell so many lies.) 2. Mek im av a chaance fe look fe it. (Let him have a chance to look for it.)

Memba: Means—remember.

1. Memba fe buy de licka fe de party. (Remember to buy the liquor [drinks] for the party.) 2. Memba fe do yu homework. (Remember to complete your homework.)

Me—naa: Means—I am not.

1. Me naa go. (I am not going.) 2. Me naa pay ten dalla fe dat. (I am not paying ten dollars ($10.00) for that.)

Me—noh: Used for—I don't.

1. Me no know weh e deh. (I do not know where it is.) 2. Me noh like im a tall. (I don't like him at all.)

Mosey or **Mosah:** Means—may be, probably, or must have.

1. She mosey lef de key pan de table. (She must have left the keys on the table.)

2. Mosey so, me no sure. (It may be so, I am not sure. It is probably so, I am not sure.)

Mout: Means—mouth.

1. Pickney, kibba yu mout. (Child, cover your mouth.) 2. Im have a big mout. (He has a big mouth.)

N

Naah: Means—not.

1. Me naah go. (I am not going.) 2. Me naah go finish me homework tenight, kauz it to much. (I am not going to finish my homework tonight, because it's too much.)

Neba or **Nebba:** Used for—never.

1. Me neba memba fe bring de pat. (I did not remember to bring the pot.) 2. She nebba even sa good night. (She never even said good night.)

Neegle: Means—needle.

1. Bring me de neegle an tread weh me lef pon de table. (Bring me the needle and thread that I left on the table.) 2. Mine yu tick yuself wid de neegle. (Be careful not to stick yourself with the needle.)

Ness: Means—nest.

1. Look! The fowl de pon the ness wid de six eggs. (Look! The fowl is sitting on the nest with the six eggs.) 2. No mash up the bird ness. (Don't break up the bird's nest.)

Nex: Used for—next or another.

1. Me we tek a nex drink fe de road. (I will take another drink [before I go] for the road.) 2. The nex time im call yu names, no ansa im. (The next time he calls you names, do not answer him.)

Noh: Means—don't, doesn't, or does not.

1. Me noh no. (I don't know.) 2. She noh waan fe go. (She does not want to go.)

Nize: Means—noise.

1. Wha mek dem a mek so much nize? (Why are they making so much noise?) 2. De loud nize a mek me ed urt. (The loud noise is making my head hurt.)

Nuff: Means—plenty of or a lot of.

1. Im lazy kaase im fambly ha nuff money. (He is lazy because his family has a lot of money.) 2. Put nuff gravy pon de rice. (Put plenty of gravy on the rice.)

Nutten: Used for—nothing.

1. The bag no heavy cause nutten much no in deh. (The bag is not heavy, because not much is in it.) 2. Nutten no in deh. (There is nothing in it.)

Nyam: Means—eat, ate, or to eat.

1. Dat mawga daag nyam a lat a de food. (That meager dog ate a lot of the food.) 2. Wa mek yu nyam soo much? (Why do you eat so much?)

O

Oba or **Ova:** Used for—over.

1. Bring de broom to sweep oba ya. (Bring the broom to sweep over here.) 2. Im no oba dear. (He is not over there.)

Onda: Means—under. Used also for Honda vehicles.

1. Look! Waan lizad deh onda de table. (Look! There is a lizard under the table.)

2. Mr. Green buy a bran new onda car. (Mr. Green bought a brand new Honda car.)

Ongle: Means—only.

1. E tek ongle a hour fe get dear. (It only takes an hour to get there.) 2. Ongle de baby and me sleep inna de ouse last night. (Only the baby and I slept in the house last night.)

Ooman: Means—woman.

1. Me bredda married a nice ooman. (My brother married a nice woman.) 2. What a pretty, little ooman? (What a pretty, little woman?)

Oonu: Used for—all of you or you.

1. Oonu please stop de nize. (All of you please stop the noise.)

2. Wa mek oonu talk so much? (Why do you talk so much?)

Ooo: Means—who.

1. Ooo was driving de truck dat ad de reck? (Who was driving the truck that had the wreck?) 2. Yu know ooo de police came fa? (Do you know who the police came for?)

Ouse: Means—house or one's dwelling place.

1. Fe yu ouse look lacka backra ouse. (Your house looks like a rich person's house.) 2. Dem lack up de ouse and move away. (They locked up the house and moved away.)

P

Pickney: Used for—child or children.

1. Wa mek de pickney tek so long fe come back? (Why does the child takes so long to return?) 2. The pickney dem is jus too nizey. (The children are just too noisy.)

Pose: Used for—a post in a fence, or to mail or post a letter or package.

1. No feget fe pose de letter. (Do not forget to mail or post the letter.) 2. De fence pose a fall dung. (The fence post is falling down.)

Priars: Means—prayers.

1. Yu must say yu priars before yu go to bed. (You are to say your prayers before you go to bed.) 2. De group leader close de meeting with priars. (The group leader closed the meeting with prayers.)

Q

Quashie: Used to describe a stupid or ignorant person.

1. De quashie dem can't even use de microwave. (Those stupid people cannot even use the microwave oven.) 2. Aal a dem a quashi. (All of them are ignorant or stupid.)

R

Rada: Means—rather or prefer.

1. Me rada no go to dat dance tenight. (I would rather not go to that dance tonight.)
2. Im rada me dan yu. (He prefers me to, or more than you.)

Rackstone: Used for—a rock.

1. No fling de rackstone ina de pool. 2. (Do not throw the rock in the pool.) 2.Tek aal de rackstone outa de hole before yu put de plant in deh. (Take all the rocks out of the hole before you put the plant in it.)

Raily: Means—really.

1. Me raily no waan fe wear dat deh dress to de wedding. (I really do not want to wear that dress to the wedding.) 2. She raily get pon me nerve. (She really gets on my nerve.)

Renk: Means—rude and/or obnoxious.

1. What a renk lickle bwoy? (What a rude little boy?) 2. Dat deh gal is very renk. (That girl is very obnoxious.)

Rhaatid: Used as an exclamation. For example Gosh! and Woh!

1. Rhaatid! Weh yu get dat? (Gosh, where did you get that?)

2. Rhaatid! Dat a waan stush chile. (Woh! That is a fantastic girl, or woman.)

Rydim: Means—rhythm, especially in walking and dancing.

1. Dat ooman gat rydim. (That woman has rhythm.) 2. Play some music wid rydim. (Play some music that has rhythm.)

S

Salve: Used for—solve, or to solve.

1.Me a de ungle one ina de class dat couda salve all a de mats problems. (I am the only one in the class that could solve all of the math problems.) 2. Rhaatid! Me kaan salve dis ya problem attall. (Gosh! I cannot solve this problem at all.)

Satcherday or Satiday: Used for—Saturday.

1. De bus leaving early Satcherday maaning. (The bus will be leaving early on Saturday morning.) 2. Me daata a come home an Satiday. (My daughter will be coming home on Saturday.)

Seh: Used interchangeably with say, said, and that.

1. She seh dat yu haffi go get yu sista from school. (She said that you have to go and get your sister from school.) 2. Tell

me madda seh me no waan fe go. (Tell my mother that I don't want to go.)

Shedule: Used for—schedule.

1. Me shedule fe wok tomarrow. (I am schedule to work tomorrow.) 2. Im sa me no deh pan de Friday shedule. (He says that I am not on Friday's schedule.)

Sinting: Means—something or thing.

1. Oh Laad! What a sinting? (Oh Lord! What a something?) 2. Arr pet pig is a ugly lickle, pat belly, sinting. (Her pet pig is an ugly little, pot bellied, thing.)

Soke: Means—to make a mess of, to do harm to another, or to interfere with someone.

1. A gwaan soke im. (I am going to do him harm or evil.) 2. She raily soke up me dress. (She really made a mess of my dress.) 3. Im is always soking wid me. (He is always interfering with me.)

Strick: Used for—strict.

1. Dat a wan strick teacha. (That is one strict teacher.) 2. No mess wid arr, kaase arr madda very strick. (Don't mess with her, because her mother is very strict.)

Sumady: Means—somebody or a person.

1. Dat a waan good sumady. (That is a good person.) 2. Dat a who me wooda call one kine sumady. (That is who I would call a kind person.)

Swimps: Means—shrimps, but also used for crawfish.

1. She a cook fry rice an swimps fe dinna. (She is cooking fried rice and shrimps for dinner.) 2. Me av a good catch a swimps lass night. (I had a good catch of shrimps last night.)

T

Tan: Means—stay.

1. No tan too lang a de hospital. (Do not stay too long at the hospital.) 2. She get a beetin kauz she tan too lang at arr fren house. (She got a spanking because she stayed too long at her friend's house.)

Tandeh: Used for—stay there.

1. Yu tandeh tink me a go wait fe yu. (You stay there thinking that I am going to wait for you.) 2. She ha fe tandeh till me come back. (She has to stay there until I return.)

Tankful: Means—thankful.

1. Me tankful to Gad dat me kan pay me bills. (I am thankful to God that I can pay my bills.) 2. Tell me wha yu thankful fa. (Tell me what you are thankful for.)

Tanks: Means—thanks.

1. Wateva de situatian we fe giv tanks. (Whatever the situation, we are to give thanks.) 2. Tell im dat me sa fe tell im tanks. (Tell him that I say to tell him thanks.)

Taut: Used for—thought.

1. Me taut im did cum back arredy. (I thought he had returned already. 2. Me taut yu say me fe put it oba deh so. (I thought you said that I should put it over there.)

Teacha: Used for—teacher.

1. De teacha say me fe mek yu sign me kansent farm. (The teacher said that I should have you sign my consent form.) 2. She a wan good teacha. (She is one good teacher.)

Tedeh or **Teday:** Means—today.

1. Yu naan go a work tedah? (Aren't you going to work today?)

2. Me son a go tek im exam tedeh. (My son will be taking his exams today.)

Tek: Means—take or to take.

1.Tek it weh fram im. (Take it away from him.) 2. No mek im tek it dung from dere. (Don't allow him to take it down from there.)

Tekeere: Means—take care.

1. Tekeere a yu baby. (Take care of your baby.) 2. O.K., tekeere, we miss yu. (O.K., take care, we miss you.)

Togedda: Used for—together.

1. Aal a we get de same grades kaase we study togedda. (All of us got the same grades, because we studied together.) 2.

Come jine unnu ands togedda to farm a circle. (Come and join your hands together to form a circle.)

Trace: Means to curse at, or to curse back at someone.

1. De gal trace me off yesseday. (The girl [or woman] cursed at me yesterday).

2. A hope me no haffi trace arr off. (I hope that I don't have to [curse her off] curse at her.)

Tree: Means—three.

1. De tree a dem climb de mango tree. (It was three of them that climbed the mango tree.) 2. De tree a dem was inna de car togedda. (The three of them got into the car together.)

Tun: Used for—turn or turned.

1. Me tun back kauz me wooda get deh too late. (I turned back, because I would

have got there too late. 2. Tun round an mek me see how de skirt fit a de back. (Turn around and let me see how the skirt fits in the back.)

U

Unifarm: Means—uniform. Usually refers to the dress code of students and health professionals.

1. Me no buy me unifarm yet. (I did not buy my uniform as of yet.) 2. De bwoys must wear brown khaki pants and white shirt fe unifarm. (The boys must wear brown khaki pants and white shirt as uniform.)

Unnu: Used for—all of you, or you are.

1. Unnu bring de bags so me kan put de food inna dem. (All of you, bring the bags so that I can put the food in them.) 2. Unnu a tell lies. (You are telling lies.)

Up: Used to emphasize proportion.

1. De tenants bruk up de house. (The tenants ruined, or "broke up" the house.)

2. No feel up de mango dem, kaase dem we get too saff. (Do not consistently feel or touch the mangoes, because they will become too soft.)

V

Vencha: Used for—attempt or attempted.

1. Me vencha fe see me baby, but de ooman sa me naan seim. (I attempted to see my baby, but the woman said I was not going to see him.) 2. Im always vencha fe learn new sinting. (He always attempts to learn something new.)

Vex: Means—to be angry, or to get angry.

1. Dat man mek me so vex me couda buss. (That man made me so angry I could burst.) 2. No worry yuself, me no vex wid yu. (Don't worry yourself, I am not angry with you.)

W

Wa: *Means—what.*

1. Wa dat? (What is that?) 2. A wa yu a sa? (What are you saying?) Sa wa? Me kaan ear yu. (Say what? I cannot hear you.)

Waan: Means—want.

1. Me no waan fe go to school teday. (I don't want to go to school today.) 2. She say dat she no waan fe se yu. (She said that she does not want to see you.)

Wan: Used for—one, or a.

1. Which wan a unnu tek de money aff de table? (Which one of you took the money off the table?) 2. Ungle wan a dem tan oba deh till it dark. (Only one of them stayed over there until it was dark.)

Waise: Used for—waist or waste.

1. What a small waise line yu ha? (What a small waist you have?) 2. Yu raily should nat waise de waata. (You really should not waste the water.)

Wamek: Means—why.

1. Wamek yu no feed de baby before yu go? (Why don't you feed the baby before you go?) 2. She sa she no know wamek yu vex wid arr. (She said she does not know why you are angry with her.)

Wata or **waata:** Means—water.

1. Bwile de wata before yu drink it, kauz it may be kantaminate. (Boil the water before you drink it, because it may be contaminated.) 2. Pour some hat waata inna de bowl. (Pour some hot water into the bowl.)

Whe: Used for—where.

1. Whe u deh? (Where are you?) 2. Me no know whe im deh. (I don't know where he is.)

Wid: Means—with.

1. Mek me go wid yu. (Let or allow me to go.) 2. Memba fi bring de money fi de book. (Remember to bring the money for the book.)

Wis: Used in comparison to a vine, or vine-like twig.

1. Go bring me piece a wis mek me tie up de bag. (Go and bring me a piece of vine to tie the (opening of) the bag.) 2. Arr waise fayva wis. (Her waist is as small as a vine.)

Wutless: Means—worthless, or of little value.

1. Wamek she married dat deh wutless man? (Why did she marry that worthless man?) 2. Demya money a wutless money so dem kaan buy much. (These monies are of little value, so they cannot buy much.)

X

Xstray or Estray: Used for—X ray.

1. De dacta seh me we haffi get estray fi diagnose wamek me a feel de pain. (The doctor said that I will have to get x-rays to help to diagnose the cause of the pain.)

2. Wa kine a xstray dem ago gi yu? (What kind of x-ray are you going to get?)

Y

Ya or **Ya so:** Used for—here.

1. No badda bring it ova (oba) ya. (Don't worry to bring it over here.) 2. She seh dat yu mus come ova ya now. (She says that you must come over here now.)

Yeye: Means—eye(s).

1. O Lawd! De fly get inna me yeye. (Oh Lord! The fly got into my eye.) 2. Opun yu yeye mek me blow it out fe yu. (Open your eye and let me blow it out for you.)

Z

Zed: Used for—Z, the last letter of the English alphabet.

1. De lickle bwoy know de alphebet fram A to Zed. (The little boy knows the alphabet from A to Z.) 2. Can yu tell me a word dat begin wid Zed? (Can you tell me a word that starts with Z?)

Teresa P Blair is a Jamaican born United States citizen, who has resided in the United States of America for over twenty five years. She migrated to the United States as an adult, and obtained her Masters degree at Central Connecticut State University, and her Ph. D. from Capella University.

She has been an educator for over 30 years, teaching from the elementary through to the college level.

She loves to teach, sing, do Bible studies, go to the beach, and watch "clean" movies. She presently resides in Georgia, where she lives with her 17 years old adopted daughter. She loves her church family and can be seen in church fellowship with them whenever the opportunity arises.